the
humble
art of
zen-cleansing
by michael de jong

clean

joost elffers books

Sterling Publishing Co., Inc.
New York

Library of Congress Cataloging-in-Publication Data Available

10 9 8 7 6 5 4 3 2 1

Published by Sterling Publishing Co., Inc. and Joost Elffers Books LLC
387 Park Avenue South, New York, NY 10016
© 2007 by Michael De Jong and Joost Elffers Books
Text © 2007 by Michael De Jong
CLEAN logo © Michael De Jong and Joost Elffers Books
Design by Yumi Asai at Berrymatch LLC
Distributed in Canada by Sterling Publishing
c/o Canadian Manda Group, 165 Dufferin Street
Toronto, Ontario, Canada M6K 3H6
Distributed in the United Kingdom by GMC Distribution Services
Castle Place, 166 High Street, Lewes, East Sussex, England BN7 1XU
Distributed in Australia by Capricorn Link (Australia) Pty. Ltd.
P.O. Box 704, Windsor, NSW 2756, Australia

Printed in China

Sterling ISBN-13: 978-1-4027-4766-3
        ISBN-10: 1-4027-4766-7
For information about custom editions, special sales, premium and
corporate purchases, please contact Sterling Special Sales
Department at 800-805-5489 or specialsales@sterlingpub.com.

CLEAN is dedicated to my Richard,
who I can bet will probably never use this book.

The Five Zen-Cleansing Ingredients

Baking Soda

Borax

Lemon

Salt

White Vinegar

A to Z Cleaning Key   ii
....

Preface   17
....

Clean (The Humble Art of Zen-Cleansing)   21
....

  Baking Soda   31
....

  Borax   57
....

  Lemon   65
....

  Salt   73
....

  White Vinegar   85
....

Zen-Cleansing Recipes   114
....

	baking soda	borax	lemon	salt	white vinegar	pages
A						
Air freshener			x	x		118
All-purpose liquid cleaner		x			x	122
Aluminum	x					39
Aluminum pots			x			72
Antiperspirant residue					x	112
Ants					x	112
Ashtray odor	x					51
Auto-body chrome	x				x	52,95
Auto-body paint	x					52
B						
Baby clothes: odors	x					50-51
Bakeware		x				64
Baking pan	x					55
Basin cleaner		x	x			123
Bath stains		x	x			122
Bathroom cleanser		x	x			63,120,123

	baking soda	borax	lemon	salt	white vinegar	pages
Bathroom sink		x	x		x	105,123
Bathtub		x	x		x	105,123
Bleach substitute		x				60
Bloodstains	x					44
Book deodorizer	x					37
Brass				x	x	124
Bugs	x					52

C

	baking soda	borax	lemon	salt	white vinegar	pages
Car: all-purpose cleanser	x					52
Car deodorizer					x	106
Car windows	x				x	52, 95
Carpets: grease	x					44
mud	x					44
odors	x					44
urine					x	94
Cast iron	x					39
Cat bedding	x					50

	baking soda	borax	lemon	salt	white vinegar	pages
Cat box	x					50
Ceramic tile: cleanser					x	105
mildew	x					42
China	x	x			x	39, 64, 101
Chopping block	x				x	120
Chrome	x				x	52, 95
Cigarette odors	x				x	51, 104, 110
Closet deodorizer	x					34
Cloth diapers: odors	x					50-51
Coffee cup	x			x		55, 81
Coffeemaker					x	104
Coffeepot	x			x		55, 81
Coffee stains	x			x		55, 79, 81
Containers: odors					x	110
stains	x		x		x	124
Cooking odors					x	103
Copper			x	x		124
Corian® counters					x	109

	baking soda	borax	lemon	salt	white vinegar	pages
Countertop: ink stain	x		x			42
Crayon	x					46
Crystal					x	101
Cutting board			x	x	x	68, 82, 98
D						
Deck: weathering	x					41
Deodorant residue					x	112
Diaper pail	x					39
Disinfectant		x				63
Dishwasher					x	101
Dishwasher soap	x	x			x	116
Dishes					x	98, 110
Dog bedding	x					50
Drain: deodorizing	x				x	34, 96
unclogging	x			x	x	79, 116
Driveway oil	x					51

	baking soda	borax	lemon	salt	white vinegar	pages
E						
Enamel	×					39
F						
Fabric: softener	×			×		50,81
brightener	×		×	×		71,123
Fiberglass	×					39
Fish odor			×	×		117
Floors	×					41
Floral longevity					×	117
Formica surfaces	×		×		×	109,120
Freezer deodorizer	×					34
Frozen pipes				×		84
Fruit: cleaning	×					41
stains					×	98
Furniture polish			×			116

	baking soda	borax	lemon	salt	white vinegar	pages
G						
Garage floor: oil stains	x					51
Garbage disposal: deodorize				x	x	83,99
Garlic odor	x		x	x	x	37,98,117
Grass removal					x	113
Grass stains					x	106
Glass					x	94
Glass coffeepot				x		81
Glassware		x			x	64,101
Glue					x	106
Grease fire	x			x		52,79
Grease stains	x					40,44
Grout					x	108
Grill	x					54
H						
Hair brush, comb	x					49

	baking soda	borax	lemon	salt	white vinegar	pages
Hard water deposits			x		x	72,108
Hard water spots					x	105
Hands: berry stains			x			71
fruit stains					x	98
garden soil	x		x			49
odors			x	x	x	68, 98,117
Household cleaner: all-purpose		x				63
Humidifier: odor			x			72
I						
Ink stains: cloth			x			71
countertops	x					42
Iron (electric)					x	92
J						
Jars					x	110
Jeans: softener				x		81

	baking soda	borax	lemon	salt	white vinegar	pages
K						
Kitchen cleanser	x	x				63,120
Kitchen fixtures			x	x		123
Kitchen sink			x			72
Kitchen stains		x	x			122
Kitchen surfaces: odors					x	98
purifying	x					56
Knives: odor			x		x	68,98
L						
Laminated counter	x				x	42,109
Laundry soap	x					50
Laundry: deodorizer	x					50-51
heavily soiled		x				60
prewash	x				x	50,121
smoke damage	x		x		x	121
soap booster	x					50
soap residue				x		81

	baking soda	borax	lemon	salt	white vinegar	pages
softener	x			x		50,81
yellowing	x			x		123
Lint					x	108
M						
Microwave	x				x	40,102
Mildew remover	x	x			x	42,122
Mineral deposits				x	x	118
Mirrors					x	94
Mud flaps	x					52
O						
Oil stains: driveway	x					51
garage floor	x					51
Onion odor	x		x	x		37,98,117
Oven grease buildup	x		x		x	103,117
Oven spill				x		76

x

	baking soda	borax	lemon	salt	white vinegar	pages
P						
Paintbrushes					x	92
Paint odors					x	110
Pans	x	x			x	64,102,123
Pantyhose				x		82
Patent leather					x	91
Pet urine					x	94
Perspiration stains	x					39
Plastic storage container	x		x		x	124
Plastic toys	x					46
Pressing creases					x	92
Porcelain	x		x	x		39,123
Pots		x	x		x	64,72,102
R						
Refrigerator: deodorizer	x	x	x			34,64,121
cleaner		x			x	64,99
Roof rack	x					52

	baking soda	borax	lemon	salt	white vinegar	pages
Room deodorizer			x			68
Rugs: grease	x					44
mud	x					44
odors	x					44
urine					x	94
Rust	x		x	x	x	36,106,118
S						
Salt stains					x	112
Scouring pad rust	x					36
Scuffs	x					40
Septic tank	x					41
Shoes: deodorize	x					54
salt stains					x	112
Shower curtain				x	x	79,113
Shower door and stall					x	105
Silk flowers				x		84
Silver	x					56

	baking soda	borax	lemon	salt	white vinegar	pages
Skunk odors					x	96
Skin softener	x					49
Smoke					x	95,104
Smoke damage	x		x		x	121
Spot remover: all-purpose			x	x		122
Soap film					x	89
Soap scum					x	105,112
Soapsuds removal				x		81
Stainless steel	x				x	39,101
Static cling					x	91
Stuffed animals	x					46
Surface cleaner: all-purpose	x					39
T						
Tarnish	x					56
Tea cups	x					55
Teapot	x				x	55,99
Tea stains					x	55

	baking soda	borax	lemon	salt	white vinegar	pages
Tile: cleanser	×	×	×		×	39,105,123
mildew	×					42
Toilet bowl: cleanser		×				63
deodorizer	×	×			×	63,117
Tools: rust					×	106
Tree sap	×					52
Tub cleaner		×	×			123
Tub			×		×	105,123
U						
Upholstery: deodorizer	×					52
grease stains	×					40
Urine odor					×	89,94
V						
Vase				×	×	118
Vegetables	×					41
Vinyl	×					52

	baking soda	borax	lemon	salt	white vinegar	pages
W						
Wall cleaner	x					46
Wallpaper: cleaner	x					36
remover					x	91
Washing machine					x	103, 112
Weed removal					x	113
Windows					x	94
Window defroster					x	95
Windshield glass	x					52, 95
Wine stains				x		83
Wok				x		76
Wooden cutting board				x	x	82, 98
Wool sweaters					x	113
Y						
Yellowed cotton and linen	x			x		123

Preface

In 1987, I moved to New York to become an artist. I had just finished graduate school and had high hopes and expectations of what life as an artist in a big city might be like. Thank God I was so naive, or I might not have done it in the first place. With a cat and a single piece of luggage filled to capacity, surprisingly I found a small apartment on the Lower East Side. I set up a little studio in the apartment and began making work. Even more surprisingly, I found a gallery to exhibit in (and another to be the director of) in record time. My first one-person show opened just five months after I arrived, and after plenty of sales and promising reviews, I quit my full-time job to become an artist.

That was also when I began cleaning apartments for extra cash to supplement my income from the sales of my art. I'd never done this before, but my plan allowed me to paint in the morning and to clean in the afternoon. I placed an ad in a newspaper advertising myself as a male housekeeper who cleaned in the "European Tradition"— whatever that meant. But it sounds convincing, doesn't it? Forty-five responses from the ad offered me a solid group of people to interview. I set up appointments carrying an attaché case (empty, of course) and wearing a crisp shirt and tie to meet clients and see which homes were, in fact, the smallest and easiest to clean. I probably don't need to tell you that most of the responses were from wackos. It is New York after all. One prospective client actually greeted me at his door naked and tried to encourage me to join him in his newfound nudist freedom.

In the end I managed to find only four individuals who were sincere—and infinitely cleaner than I would ever dream of being. And so I began traveling the subways from the Cloisters to the World Trade Center, going from apartment to apartment with a homemade cleaning kit of commercially manufactured scouring powders and surface cleaners, paper towels, garbage bags, rags, and whatnot. I wasn't sure of what I needed, or frankly of what I was doing, but as a child I had watched my mom wash and vacuum the floor, wipe down the counters, and scour the bathroom. Since I had inherited her addiction to cleanliness and used it in my college dorm rooms and now my own little hovel, I figured I could do it for others.

I cleaned with abandon. Bleach-infused powder filled the air while I sprayed grease-cutting agents to quickly clean, deodorize, and disinfect. Glass cleaners hovered and oven cleaners fumed as I vacuumed, laundered, wiped, and polished. The windows shined and surfaces sparkled. Beds had military corners and dust bunnies were exterminated. Closets were organized, and slipcovers, walls, and even lampshades were restored to their original cleanliness. The effect was dazzling.

I, however, felt like hell. It was then that I came to realize that the overexposure to household cleaning products was robbing me of my health.

Since I couldn't afford to quit, I needed a solution, and this is how I came by it. I began to consider that, perhaps, cleaning products needn't always come from the hardware or grocery store. Pioneers traveled across the plains without handy wipes, dishwasher tabs, or self-sanitizing lotion. And had it not been for the fact that they were probably trampled by their own livestock, killed by each other, or didn't pack enough rations for their travels, most would have arrived at their destination hardy, healthy, and clean.

No matter how you look at it, cleaning is hard work. I'm not going to tell you I have a magic solution that will make cleaning a breeze. And there are certainly ways of making any cleaning chore easier, but using commercial cleaning products is not the solution. These may work well on your countertop—but they could also send you into cardiac arrest. And honestly, they don't actually work so well. After seven years of cleaning professionally, I can attest to that. Now I have come to think that cleaning with wholesome ingredients is not an alternative but the solution. It's cheaper, healthier, easier, and it's infinitely more effective.

CLEAN (The Humble Art of Zen-Cleansing)
... or how to become your own cleaning Buddhist.

"Cleanliness is indeed next to godliness."

(John Wesley, circa 1760)

Okay, the truth of the matter is most people hate to clean. It's a necessary evil, and even then most folks find ways of avoiding it—or simply get someone else to do it for them. However, I'll admit to being the weirdo in the crowd who, on many levels, truly enjoys cleaning.

I actually move the fridge when I vacuum. Not what the average housekeeper might do, but that's just me. (It's a little obsessive, I admit—OK, a lot obsessive—but you'd be surprised what you find hiding, or worse yet, lurking there.) Mine is a cleaning ritual I learned from my Dutch-born mother, Ruth, and by doing it I gain peace of mind—the satisfaction of knowing that my kitchen is really clean.

My mom was my cleaning Guru! My devotion to and gratification from cleaning I owe to her. And it all surely started with the "Cleaning Game" she played with me and my siblings every Saturday morning when we were young. She somehow got us to eagerly pick three to four "special chores" from a bowl to finish before playtime. Over the years, cleaning became ingrained in me as an inspirational, almost spiritual-like exercise that brings self-satisfaction as well as happiness to those around us.

As a result, every day, I make it a habit to do just a little cleaning before leaving for work. But on Saturdays I spin like some caffeinated twister: shaking rugs until the bindings come loose; vacuuming until the machine gags from lack of suction; washing shirts that are actually going to the professional laundry on Monday; changing beds (including two guest beds whether we've had company or not); scrubbing out the sinks, tubs, and toilets; and mopping every square inch of my living space, which I share with a partner who does not have my passion for cleaning. I admit it, were I the type to have a housekeeper, I would probably clean before he or she arrived.

Occasionally my intense focus and energy succeeds in frightening my partner into a state of suspension in which he hypnotically offers his acquiescent assistance and gets caught up in my transcendental cleansing enterprises. But most times he just finds reasons to leave the house altogether—to go grocery shopping or, with our dog Jack in tow, take an extended visit to the park and local coffee shop until "it's over."

But again, that's just me. I expect this of no one. So please don't panic. This book is not about cleaning obsessions—to the contrary, it's about the mindfulness of cleaning effectively with the simplest and safest of ingredients. It's about doing what most people hate in a way that is actually healthful, thoughtful, and respectful—of yourself, your loved ones, your pets and neighbors, your environment, and your planet.

In essence, this book is about what I irreverently call "Zen-Cleansing." Many religious philosophies respect cleanliness and the act of cleaning—it's "next to Godliness" and all that. And if you think about it, it is in our spiritual nature to pursue some level of cleanliness and order. Faiths such as Islam, Christianity, Judaism, Buddhism, and Hinduism have age-old parables that speak of the humility and spiritual importance in washing, organization, and other household activities.

For instance, the closer a Buddhist comes to being one with the Universe, the more menial his or her daily tasks become. The highest-ranking monks are given the honor of cleaning up after meals. (Wow, imagine if our highest-ranking politicians and CEOs behaved similarly—actually serving citizens and consumers!) It is a Zen Buddhist spiritual goal to create inner and outward purity by achieving inner and universal harmony through applying care and mindfulness to everyday, lowly activities as if they actually mattered.

From this simple, yet somewhat difficult practice, it is implied that by cleaning with care we can allow the task to become a meaningful, transcendental experience. I must admit that in my Whirling Dervish Saturday cleaning spurts, my head is cleared, and my body and mind feel harmonized—that's why I call it "Zen-Cleansing."

Zen-Cleansing is a mindful way of letting go of the drudgery associated with cleaning, and finding your spick-and-span center—

to joyously give yourself up to cleaning. Not just spritzing, soaking, scrubbing, scouring, vacuuming, mopping, and dusting…but rather spritzing, soaking, scrubbing, scouring, vacuuming, mopping, and dusting with a concern for and a knowing oneness with the universe!

According to ancient Chinese philosophy, the universe is divided into dual energies called the yin and the yang. From the dynamic interaction of yin and yang come the five elements, or energy fields—wood, fire, earth, metal, and water—that underlie all things in nature. It is believed that the proper balance of these elements brings harmony to life; this concept even extends to Chinese cooking, which also has five elements (sour, bitter, sweet, spicy, salty). There are five elements in Zen-Cleansing and they also operate on the same yin/yang principles. In Zen-Cleansing, all of the elements are equally important. They depend on one another for an amazing chain reaction and interaction. It is the pairing, marriage, and balance of elements that makes for the spiritual, integrated experience. Each ingredient has its own place and each has its own function—both singularly and in combination with the others.

The five simple ingredients that are used in Zen-Cleansing are baking soda, borax, lemon, salt, and white vinegar. There is nothing new or unusual about any of them, and in fact, they have been used for centuries. I would wager that at least four if not all five ingredients are already in your home. They are pure, wholesome, and natural—and none will hurt (and may actually help!) you, your family, your pets, your neighborhood, and the environment.

What is truly amazing about these simple ingredients is that their combinations create catalysts for cleanliness. When a sodium substance such as salt, borax, or baking soda is exposed to an acid substance such as white vinegar or lemon, carbon dioxide (CO_2) is released. Carbon dioxide in its solid form is better known as dry ice. But no need to worry, you will never create dry ice in your home by mixing any of the five Zen-Cleansing agents. Don't expect to see the pillows of puffy white clouds or the spooky, smoky tendrils that you might recall from chemistry class, when the teacher put a chunk of dry ice in a bowl of water. And there is no need to worry about touching any of the mixtures—they cannot burn your skin the way dry ice can.

Expect something much more subtle but no less wondrous. In Zen-Cleansing, when any of the salt and acidic ingredients are joined and create carbon dioxide, miraculously surfaces are caused to cool ever so slightly, and the dirt actually pops off. I'm not "Mr. Wizard," but that's really the simplest explanation. And regardless of the chemistry, it works.

The ancient Greeks in their wisdom, and even the early American colonists in their struggles to survive, cleaned with these same basic elements—salt and acid. So perhaps in this modern age, when new toxic and wasteful cleaning products are introduced to the market on a daily basis (mindlessly enticing us with infomercials and product placements), it's a timely idea for us to rethink using salt and acid. After all, it's our homes, our health, and our environment that we're trying to keep clean. Dogen, a thirteenth-century Buddhist teacher, taught that any unused water should be returned to the stream that it came from. And any water used while Zen-Cleansing can actually be returned to the environment because the five ingredients—baking soda, borax, lemon, salt, and white vinegar—are completely safe. They harm nothing. They just clean. They are so safe, in fact, that you probably eat four of the five—baking soda, lemon, salt, and vinegar—on a daily basis. (And just in case I need to remind you, don't eat the fifth—borax. It's a mineral mined from the ground that, while not ecologically harmful, has absolutely no dietary value! And if ingested, it could make you sick. So, please, keep it out of the reach of children and pets.)

Unlike today's marketed cleansers, Zen-Cleansing ingredients will not harm your respiratory system, make you cough, give you a bloody nose, loosen your bowels, cause gout, or leave a toxic residue on your kitchen or bath surfaces. They will not pollute the air, rivers, or soil. Make no mistake, they will require the same "elbow grease" as commercial products, but they won't harm your hands, eyes, lungs, etc., and you won't need rubber gloves to avoid caustic burns. Of course, if you are the type who likes to clean in rubber gloves, by all means, go ahead.

Another thing to note is that unlike commercial products that line supermarket shelves in colorful and alluring packaging, Zen-Cleansing ingredients require only simple packaging that you can supply yourself. Empty plastic spray bottles or peanut butter or mayonnaise jars (that you probably already have or might even "rescue" from a neighbor's recycling bin) will work perfectly. In fact, just by involving yourself in this simple recycling act, think of all the plastic packaging that will no longer need to be manufactured and thus won't find its non-biodegradable way into landfills or recycling centers across the country.

So, in addition to being a simple and effective way to clean the toughest dirt, Zen-Cleansing is also an environmentally sane alternative to the prepackaged goods in grocery and hardware stores. Just look through your pantry and refrigerator for what you'll need—you probably already have most of the items on hand. Just think, if we don't buy toxic cleaning products, then we won't use them. And if we don't use them, there's no real reason to make them. The reality is that we really didn't need any of them in the first place, but we've been brainwashed into thinking that we did.

Having said all that, Zen-Cleansing is a philosophy, a cleaning guide, and a book about cleaning that might just start a revolution. Maybe it's how we reclaim the environment, put big business in its place, and make it safe again not just for our children, loved ones, and pets, but for everything that climbs, crawls, flies, or swims. Think of it as a way of being one with the universe on a daily basis, and doing your part to make the world a safer, cleaner, more beautiful place.

The birds in the sky and the fish in the depths of the ocean leave no trace of their passing (OK, they do poop, and sometimes on us!)—and we should take note. In essence, your mind and your environment are one. Open your awareness to your actions in order to benefit the good of every other thing. In Zen, we meet ourselves in whatever task we take on. Whatever we see, whatever we hear, whatever we smell, taste, or touch, we end up experiencing as ourselves. In Zen-Cleansing, we meet ourselves in the mindful act of safely and purely cleaning our personal environment.

Your environment, your daily activities and your inner thoughts are one and tell the world who you are…even if you are a messed up, clean-obsessed freak like me. So let us wield our cleaning cloths with honor. Refrigerator-movers of the world unite!

[And, dear reader, although cleaning is never "easy," I've made accessing and finding cleaning recipes and "How Tos" a lot easier with a handy, user-friendly key at the beginning of this book.]

baking soda

Introduction to Baking Soda

Fresh from the box, its finely formed crystals sparkle like a freshly fallen snow. White, powdery, and soft to the touch, odorless and inert upon inspection, the lonely baking soda loiters endlessly in the fridge, in the shadows behind leftovers, lunchmeat, and lettuce.

From the ashes of burnt corncobs, pioneers made early baking sodas named saleratus, trona, or niter (natron). Found on the shelves of frontier homes as well as in the traveling medicine man's bag of talismans and herbs, it was prescribed as a cure for everything from asthma to eczema and bellyaches. It transformed animal fat into treatments for chapped skin and did double duty to clean floors, scrub pots, and shine shoes.

Cleaning and bathing with baking soda goes back to biblical times. "For though thou wash with nitre, and take thee much soap, yet thine iniquity is marked before me, saith the Lord God" (Jeremiah 2:22). Perhaps this verse implies that even with soap and ash as our purifiers, only God can wash away our transgressions.

Baking soda or natron is a naturally occurring substance, created from the evaporation of lake water in hot desert climates. Natron has been discovered in the tombs of the Valley of the Kings; it was used by the ancient Egyptians as a key ingredient in the art of mummification. Superior as a drying agent because it chemically destroys grease and fat, natron has also been found as a residue in the mummies themselves. Crystals from the famous natron beds of Egypt have been traded for thousands of years. Egyptian writings as old as the reign of Ramses III (ca. 12th century B.C.) refer to these deposits.

Sprinkled, scattered, spread, or strewn, kept in your closet, kitty litter, or carport—baking soda, in any of its guises, is powerful enough to preserve the dead. (Not a "do-it-yourself" project!) Yet, it also has the sparkling ability to sweeten, clean, and freshen your home. Baking soda is the most effective, most useful, and most used element of the five Zen-Cleansing ingredients.

• Baking soda works great as a freshener and deodorizer in the **freezer**, in the **refrigerator**, and in the **closet**. Just tear the top off a new box of baking soda and let it do its thing. After a month, replace the old container with a fresh one and recycle the old box in a cleaning project to dispose of it. You can also pour some baking soda down your **drain** to keep it free of odors.

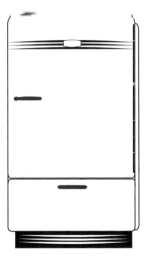

• Try spot cleaning **wallpaper** by making a paste of baking soda and water. (A paste may be made by adding a few drops of water to a quarter cup of baking soda. The finished product should resemble the consistency of toothpaste.) Wipe it on with a soft cloth and attempt to remove the soil or spot using a slow, methodical, circular motion. Follow by wiping again with a clean, lightly dampened cloth. This will require a delicate hand, some patience, and the ability to say, "Enough is enough."

• By adding baking soda to your **scouring pad**, you may prevent it from rusting.

- Place musty **books**, old or new, into a plastic bag with baking soda to eliminate mildew and stinky odors. Allow it to absorb the odors and mildew (or until the offending smell has disappeared). The process may take a few weeks.

- To rid your **hands** of **odors**, like **onions** or even **garlic**, quickly scrub with baking soda and water. Use a nailbrush, if you think you need to, and then rinse with warm running water.

- For tough surface stains: in a medium-size bowl, add one-half box of baking soda and enough water until the baking soda is the consistency of cake batter. Use it to scour **tiles**, **fiberglass**, **fine china**, **porcelain**, **enameled surfaces**, **stainless steel**, **aluminum**, and even **cast iron**. Scrub, rinse, and wipe dry. The scouring mixture should keep for a few days if stored in a covered, airtight container.

- Rub a spoonful of baking soda-water paste into a **perspiration stain**. Really unfortunate stains may need to sit for an hour or two. Wash as usual.

- A cup of baking soda sprinkled into your **baby's diaper pail** will keep it smelling fresh (er?).

• Zap away **microwave stains**. Put two or three spoons of baking soda into one cup of water and boil it for two minutes in your microwave. The steam from the boiling baking soda-infused water will soften even the hardest, greasiest, yuckiest, baked-on messes. Wipe clean.

• A paste of baking soda and water is gentle enough to remove **shoe** and **furniture scuffs** on all kinds of flooring.

• Sprinkle baking soda on **fabric** and **silk** upholstery to absorb even the greasiest stains. Don't work it in, but just let it sit overnight and then vacuum the baking soda up.

40

- Add two cups of baking soda to a gallon of water and swab onto your new **deck** to give it a weathered look instantly.

- Add one-half cup of baking soda to a bucket of water to mop **floors**. Mop as usual, rinse, and wipe dry.

- Place a cup of baking soda every week down your toilet or drain to help maintain the pH balance of your **septic tank** and to keep it flowing smoothly.

- Rinse **pesticides**, **dirt**, and **wax** from fruit and vegetables by adding a few tablespoons of baking soda to a sink of warm water. Rinse the produce with clean water, pat dry, display and, of course, devour.

- Remove **scratches** and **cuts** from **laminated counters** by cleaning with a baking soda-water paste. Rub in a circular motion and watch marks disappear. Be prepared to contribute some elbow grease.

- Remove **ink stains** left by price tags or plastic bags on **countertops** with a baking soda-water paste. For old or stubborn stains, apply lemon juice first.

- Make a **tile cleanser** that will remove even tough **mildew stains** by mixing two cups of baking soda and a half-cup of lukewarm water. Use an old toothbrush or household brush to work it into the grout and scrub, scrub, scrub. Rinse with warm water.

42

- Sprinkle a fresh **mud spot** on your **carpet** or **rug** with enough baking soda to cover completely. Let stand for 20 minutes and then vacuum.

- Similarly, cover **grease spots** in your rug with baking soda. Let it sit for one hour, scrub with a dry brush, and then vacuum.

- If your **carpets** and **rugs** smell musty, sprinkle a thin layer of baking soda over the entire surface. Let sit overnight, and then vacuum.

- Remove **bloodstains** from color-safe **fabrics** by rinsing them with cold water, then sprinkling baking soda on the area. Rub the fabric into itself and run under cool water again.

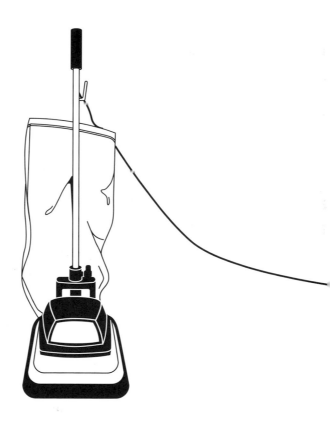

Vacuum 'til the cord tells you to stop.

- To clean your child's **stuffed animals**, pour a cup of baking soda into a large, clean plastic bag. Place the toys into the bag and shake. Remove the toys and shake them over the garbage can to remove the remaining powder. Vacuum if necessary.

- Clean solid **plastic toys** with three tablespoons of baking soda dissolved into a quart of warm water. Dip a sponge into the solution and rub it over the toys. Use a clean, damp cloth to rinse.

- Baking soda can remove **crayon** from **walls** and even from **launderable** items. Place one-cup baking soda in the wash and run as usual. To remove crayon from walls, make a paste and scrub. Rinse with clean water. (Note: If the crayon doesn't come out of a fabric, wash it again before you place it in the dryer, otherwise the heat could set the wax and color in for good.)

- Try adding a half-teaspoon of baking soda to a sink full of water and soak your **hair combs** and **brushes**. It will remove hair spray and oils in just a few minutes.

- Add just a half-cup of baking soda to your bath water to make your **skin softer** than it's ever been.

- For really **dirty gardener's hands**, a generous lump of baking soda mixed into a paste and scrubbed with a nailbrush will make your hands clean—and soft. The soil already makes a meal of your hands and cuticles, why should your hand soap, too?

- To boost your **laundry soap**, **soften** your **clothes**, and deodorize an entire load of **laundry**, add one cup of baking soda to your automatic washing machine before adding your soap and clothes. Launder as usual.

- Keep your **cat box** smelling fresh by sprinkling baking soda into the **litter box** before adding the cat litter.

- If your **dog** or **cat bedding** is less than fresh, sprinkle baking soda onto it. Let it sit for about an hour, then vacuum.

- Add a half-cup of baking soda to a bucket of water and soak **cloth diapers** or even soiled **baby clothes** to remove **odors**. Remove from this prewash, and then launder as usual.

50

The baking soda is even safe enough for use on items that will touch a newborn's skin.

- **Fill ashtrays** in your car and home with baking soda to assist in absorbing odors and to make certain cigarettes are extinguished. (It's a filthy, nasty habit, but some folks still smoke!)

- To remove **oil** on your **driveway** or **garage floor**, sprinkle baking soda over the spots to absorb them. Add a bit of water to the baking soda to form a paste. With a brush in your hand or a scrub pad under the sole of your shoe, work it up. Rinse with soap and water, and repeat if necessary. It should get some of the spill or stains up. If not, get over it. It's a garage floor after all.

- Add a quarter cup of baking soda to a bucket of water to remove **bugs** and **tree sap** from the **chrome, windshield glass, mud flaps, auto roof rack**, and **auto-body paint** on your car. It's really effective as a scrub, too. Just apply a bit onto a rag or sponge to get the really nasty stuff up. Rinse with clean water. Try it on the **vinyl seats** inside, too.

- Sprinkle baking soda onto your **upholstered couch** or **favorite chair** to deodorize it. Let it stand for about an hour or so and then vacuum.

- Did you ever think that you could extinguish a **grease fire** with baking soda? It's true. (But let's hope you never have to put this to the test.)

- They may not be roses, but why shouldn't they smell like a dozen. Sprinkle a bit of baking soda into your **shoes** before and after wearing; **your feet** will feel cooled, and your shoes will stay fresh.

- You're planning a cookout and your **outdoor grill** is a mess! Make a paste of baking soda and water and scrub with a wire brush to remove last night's (or last summer's!) remains. You'll need a bit of elbow grease to get it shiny. Rinse and repeat until clean.

- Sprinkle baking soda directly into your **garbage**. This will make it smell a lot fresher.

- Baked-on messes are easy to remove simply by placing a couple of spoonfuls of baking soda and your dish liquid into your dirty **baking pan**. Let it soak for an hour or, if necessary, overnight. Wipe it out with a cloth or a sponge. If any bits remain, make a baking soda paste and scrub the sticky bits right up. Rinse with clean water.

- Remove **coffee stains** and **tea stains** from your coffeepot, teapot, and cups by scrubbing with baking soda and a soft cloth. Rinse with water.

- Your **sterling silver** or **silverplate** will always look like you have a full staff—even if all you have is a box of baking soda. (This is amazing.) Line your kitchen sink or a wash bucket with aluminum foil. (The heavy-duty stuff works best.) Load up the silver you intend to polish, making certain that each item touches the foil liner. Cover the entire contents with boiling water and add a cup of baking soda. The **tarnish** jumps from the silver to the foil in almost no time at all! For heavy tarnish that may still remain, make a paste of water and baking soda and polish those surfaces 'til they shine.

- If you insist on using potentially toxic cleansers, after doing so, please clean all of your **kitchen surfaces** with baking soda to make certain that no cleaning chemicals end up in your food.

56

borax

Introduction to Borax

Borax (Zen-Cleansing's second ingredient) is the fifth element on the periodic table of elements and lies buried deep in the Mohave Desert, the Andes, Turkey, Tibet, and Death Valley. It forms in the most arid regions of the planet. Carried by streams flowing out from the runoff of nearby mountains during wet seasons, the mineral-rich overflow becomes concentrated in temporary lakes that then evaporate in the scorched, barren desert climates. Ultimately the concentration accumulates to produce the crystals we know as borax.

For many of you, borax, like the then-still-young and ever-tanned face of Ronald Reagan, will forever be connected with the popular

television show *Death Valley Days* (1952–75). The weekly show about tales of the Old West was sponsored by 20 Mule Team® Borax, a brand founded in 1980 that is still sold today.

Borax has a color that is white to clear, and its texture is fine and powdery, silky and smooth to the touch. Slightly soluble in cold water and highly soluble in hot, it can be used as a cleaning agent, weed killer, disinfectant or, as it says on the box, to "speed and sweeten laundry."

Store borax in the container it comes in or in a sealed recycled jar, out of the reach of children and pets. Keep it in a dry place so the crystals stay light, soft, and powdery.

• Adding one-quarter cup of borax to two cups of water makes a highly effective **bleach substitute**. (The combination of borax and water acts like hydrogen peroxide.)

• For **heavily soiled clothing**, add one-half cup borax to your detergent and launder clothes as usual.

No meal's complete until a garment's been soiled.

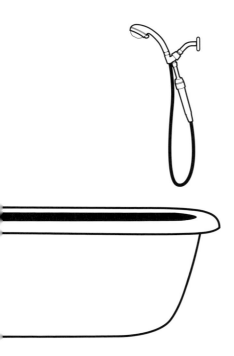

*Your tub and your spouse are the
ring bearers who know you best.*

- You can make a general, all-purpose **household cleaner** by adding one-half cup of borax to one gallon of water.

- By combining equal parts borax and hot water, you create a highly effective **disinfectant**.

- Your **bathroom** will shine when cleaned with borax. Apply to a soft cloth or a dampened sponge and use as you would an ordinary **bathroom** or **kitchen cleanser**. It can be used on any surface in the bathroom or kitchen without the risk of scratching.

- Add one-quarter cup of borax to your **toilet bowl** to help clean and deodorize it. Swish the mixture with a brush and allow to stand for at least an hour, or even better, overnight. Then just flush.

- Borax is delicate enough for your **fine china** and **glassware** as well as **pots, pans,** and **bakeware**. Add one half-cup to a sink full of water. Wash items well and rinse with clear water.

- Add one tablespoon of borax to one quart of warm water and use the mixture to clean and deodorize your **refrigerator**.

lemon

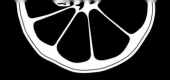

Introduction to Lemon

With sharp thorns and twigs, oblong leaves, and fragrant, reddish buds that blossom into white and lavender flowers, the lemon tree's fruit is light yellow, oval, and aromatic. The fruit's juicy, acidic segments are hidden under a leathery exterior rind, which is dotted with the oil glands that produce the lemon's memorable effervescent scent. Pungent, sharp, heady, bitter, and at times overpowering, the lemon was once prized by sultans, gifted by kings, and traded across the continents by sailors, pirates, and smugglers. Although its origin is unknown, the lemon is believed to have been cultivated in ancient Iraq and Egypt. It is rumored that Christopher Columbus carried its seeds in his vest pockets. Today the sour and succulent fruit is grown in Italy, Spain, Greece, Turkey, Cyprus, Lebanon, South Africa, Australia, the Philippines, and of course, the United States.

With dozens of varieties carrying usual names like Armstrong, Bearss, Berna, Eureka, Femminello Ovale, Genoa, Harvey, Interdonato, Lisbon, Meyer, Monachello, Nepali Oblong, Perrine, Ponderosa, Rosenberger, Santa Teresa, and Villafranca—each slightly varying in color, texture, shape, flavor, and scent—the common lemon may not be "oh-so-common" after all. Whether you choose the exotic or the mundane variety, any lemon you can get your hands on will certainly do the trick.

A bowl of a dozen lemons placed casually out in the open, another bunch tossed into your refrigerator's crisper, and perhaps a small covered dish filled with cut slices ready for the taking stashed in your refrigerator door will make living with the most perishable of the five Zen-Cleansing ingredients that much easier.

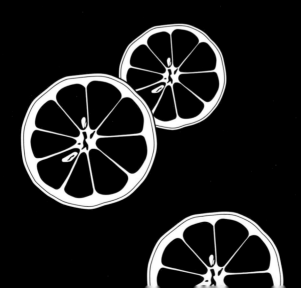

- Slice a lemon and put it into a pot of water and bring to a boil. After an hour, the lemon **aroma** should most certainly refresh your home.

- Rub fresh lemon into a **cutting board** to remove discolorations. For heavy stains, allow it to sit. Wash and rinse with clear water.

- The juice of a lemon removes the **odor of onion or garlic** from **knives** and **hands**.

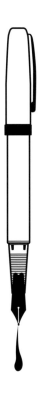

- Remove **berry stains** from your **hands** by placing a bit of lemon juice on them. Wash and rinse with clear water.

- Remove **ink stains** on cloth by placing lemon juice directly onto the spot. Allow to sit overnight before laundering as usual. Repeat if necessary before placing in the dryer.

- To **brighten** your **white fabrics**, soak them in a pot with boiling water and a sliced lemon.

- A 50-50 solution of lemon juice and water should dissolve your **hard water deposits**.

- To shine your **aluminum pots**, rub with the cut side of a lemon.

- To rid your **humidifier** of odors, add three or four caps of lemon juice to the water.

- Remove watermarks and grease from your **kitchen sink** after a big meal by adding a slice of lemon to your final rinse water.

salt

Introduction to Salt

Stored in shakers on dining tables, presented in heaping bowls, or found next to stovetops, this coarse, granular, or powdery white mineral is always on hand in a pinch, and is used to enhance almost every sweet or savory culinary invention. And it has also long served as a purifier and cleaner.

Listed on the periodic table of elements, sodium chloride in all its forms (iodized, sea, bay, kosher, canning, pickling or rock salt), occurs naturally in soil and water. Like baking soda, it too was used to preserve the remains of the ancient Pharaohs. Salt is the fourth most abundant element on earth, and it is even found in great bubbling lakes on the planet Mars.

No less than thirty references to salt are made in the Bible. (Most notably, perhaps, when Lot's wife was transformed into a cold and bloodless statue of the stuff because she defiantly turned to see the fall of Gomorrah.)

Roman soldiers of antiquity were often paid in salt, and this was called their *salarium*, from which our word "salary" is derived. It was said a soldier was "worth his salt," a term still used for a worthy person. Once paid with salt, it could be used as money in exchange for other goods.

Sprinkled over eggs, used to cure meat, or even to gargle, the plentiful common table salt can stand alone—(a pillar) among spices—and cleansers!

Zen-Cleansing with Salt

- Clean your **wok** by scrubbing it with a small amount of salt on a paper towel dampened with cooking oil.

- In the event of an **oven spill**, sprinkle salt into the mess and then scrub.

- Remove **perspiration stains** in clothing by presoaking garments in salt water.

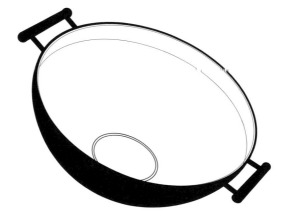

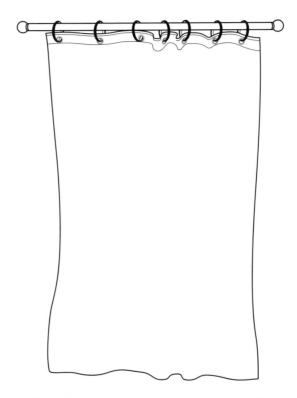

There's no reason to cultivate mildew.
It doesn't bear fruit.

- Remove fresh **coffee stains** by dousing affected areas with cold salt water.

- Remove **bloodstains** in clothing by soaking garments in cold salt water overnight. Wash as usual.

- Soak your laundered **shower curtain** in salt water. This should retard the growth of mildew.

- Salt and boiling water poured down your **drains** helps keep them flowing.

- Salt will put out a **grease fire**.

- **Soften stiff new jeans** by adding a half cup of salt and then wash along with your regular laundry detergent.

- Remove **soapsuds** from your sink by adding salt to your rinse water.

- **Soap residue** is easily removed from your laundry by adding a quarter cup of salt to your rinse cycle. This also acts as a marvelous **fabric softener**, too.

- To erase **coffee stains** from the inside of a **glass coffeepot**, add four teaspoons salt, one cup crushed ice, and one tablespoon water. Gently swirl until clean, then rinse. Note: Coffeepot should be at room temperature before cleaning.

• Eliminate **odors** from your **wooden cutting board** by applying a generous amount of salt directly onto the board. Rub firmly with the palm of your hand. This should not only remove any odors but a bit of the surface grime as well. Rinse with water.

• Prevent runs in new **pantyhose**. Wash pantyhose and allow them to drip dry. Then, mix two cups of salt with one gallon of water and soak pantyhose for three hours, rinse in cool water, and drip dry. This will make the hosiery stronger and less apt to run.

- Pour a half-cup of salt into the **garbage disposal**. Then, by running the disposal (following manufacturer's directions), you'll send any odors down the drain!

- Use salt to help remove **wine stains** from cotton fabric. Pour enough salt on the stain to soak up the liquid. Soak the fabric for a half hour in cold water. Wash as usual.

- Put your **silk flowers** into a large bag and pour in one cup of salt. Shake the contents. Your flowers are now clean.

- Pour a box of salt down each of your drains to prevent **frozen pipes** during winter months.

white vinegar

Introduction to White Vinegar

Sharp, sour, and biting . . . the flavor of vinegar, to most of us, always remains the same whether we are tasting rice, red, white, balsamic, or apple cider vinegar.

Vinegar (the word, from the French, translates as "sour wine") can be produced from assorted fruits, berries, melons, coconut, honey, beer, maple syrup, potatoes, beets, malt, grains, or whey. But the production, in essence, remains unaffected no matter what its origin—a first fermentation of sugar to alcohol, and then a second fermentation to vinegar. Voilà! Acetic acid is born.

Most major religions make references to vinegar—whether it's Confucianism, Buddhism, Taoism, or Christianity. In fact, when and how an immortal deity responded to the taste of vinegar was often used as a metaphor for that deity's view on life.

The ancients stumbled upon the versatility of vinegar probably more than 10,000 years ago. The Babylonians used it as medicine and also flavored their meals with it. The Romans drank it as a beverage. Cleopatra dissolved pearls in it to prove she could devour a fortune in a single meal. Biblical references show how vinegar was used for its soothing and healing properties, and as recently as World War I, vinegar was still being used to treat wounds in the battlefields.

Susan B. Anthony was considered the "vinegar" of the women's suffrage movement. By being aggressive, breezy, ebullient, frisky, spunky, and full of vitality, she displayed the classic traits of being full of "piss and vinegar," a phrase often used by Steinbeck in *The Grapes of Wrath*.

It's said, "You catch more flies with honey than with vinegar." So go ahead and clean with it. (Who wants to attract flies anyway?!) Store your white vinegar in a sealed container alone or dilute it 50-50 with water in a spray bottle for everyday use. There is no need for refrigeration. Vinegar's shelf life is eternal.

Zen-Cleansing with White Vinegar

- Always take a moment to recognize your materials and know your surfaces before you begin cleaning. A remarkable cleaner, white vinegar can cut **greasy film** but is strong enough to create pits and marks in marble.

- White vinegar is great for **colorfast clothes**… except for cotton and linen. Be sure to read your content labels.

- White vinegar neutralizes alkaline soaps. It can remove **soap film** when added to your laundry's final rinse cycle.

- White vinegar also breaks down stubborn **urine odors**. Add a quarter-cup to your washing machine when cleaning your baby's diapers to make them soft and sweet—for the next "go-round."

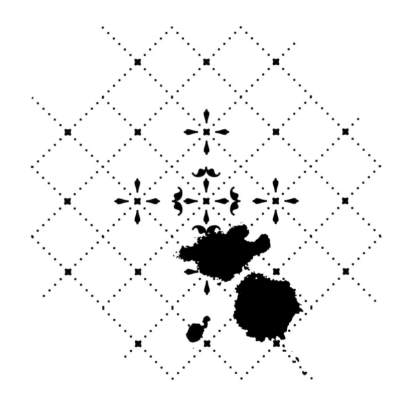

90

- You can polish **patent leather** using a cloth dampened with white vinegar. Just dab it on full strength, then gently rub and wipe off 'til the shine is fully restored.

- White vinegar works well as a **wallpaper remover**. Spray on a mixture of half water-half vinegar and allow it to soak into the paper. Begin peeling, picking, and scraping away.

- Remove **static cling** from your clothing by adding a quarter-cup of white vinegar to the final rinse cycle in your washing machine.

- You can soften hardened **paintbrushes** by placing them in hot white vinegar. Place vinegar in a glass or plastic cup in the microwave (or in a pan on the stove top) and bring it to a slow boil. Remove it from the heat source and soak your paintbrushes in it overnight.

- When rehemming clothes, sprinkle some white vinegar on the previous crease and iron over it. This will help take out the **pressing creases** to assist you in making a new hem.

- White vinegar unclogs the steam vents in an electric **iron**. Fill the reserve with vinegar and allow it to run full heat on the highest setting. Once the vents are clear, empty the iron of the excess vinegar and refill with clean water.

92

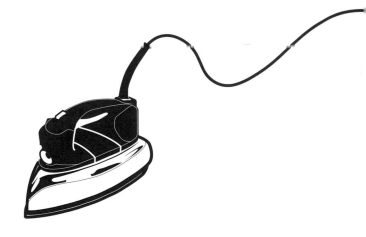

- A solution of two tablespoons of white vinegar to one gallon of warm water in a spray bottle is a great way to clean **mirrors**, **glass**, and **windows**. Spray onto the area to be cleaned and polish with recycled newspapers.

- Dilute one cup of white vinegar with one cup of room temperature water to reduce the **odor** of a **pet's urine** in your **carpeting**. Apply and blot with a clean cloth or rag.

- Fill a spray bottle with a 50-50 mixture of water and white vinegar to **deodorize** the air while you are cooking. Spritz it around and notice the difference.

- Fill a bathtub with super hot water and add a cup of white vinegar. By hanging your clothes in the white vinegar infused steam, **smoke** and **other odors** will be reduced.

- Keep your car windows frost-free with a homemade **defroster**. Coat the windshield and windows the night before with a solution of three parts white vinegar to one part water. (Don't wipe it off.) It's also a great way to clean your **car windows**.

- Polish your cars' **auto-body chrome** by applying white vinegar full strength with a soft cloth. Buff until it's shiny.

• Remove **skunk odor** from your dog. Rub Fido's fur with full-strength white vinegar and then bathe as usual. "Rinse and repeat" may well apply in this situation. (You'll probably need a bath, too, when you're done!)

• To **deodorize your kitchen drain**, pour a cup of white vinegar down the drain once a week. Let stand 30 minutes, then flush with cold water.

- Eliminate **onion** and **garlic odors** from your **hands** and from your **knives** and **kitchen surfaces** by rubbing white vinegar on them before and after slicing.

- Clean and disinfect your **wooden cutting board** by wiping with full-strength white vinegar.

- To remove **fruit stains** from hands simply rinse them with white vinegar.

- Cut through grease and odor on your **dishes** by adding a tablespoon of white vinegar to hot soapy wash water. Rinse with clean water.

- To clean a stained and soiled **teapot**, boil a 50-50 mixture of water and white vinegar in the teapot over a high flame on your stove. Dispose of the mixture and then wipe away the grime with a rag.

- Wash out your **refrigerator** with a solution of equal parts water and white vinegar. It will make everything sparkle.

- Clean and deodorize your **garbage disposal** by making white vinegar ice cubes. Feed enough cubes into the disposal to fill it, and then operate. After grinding, run cold water through the disposal to rinse it clean.

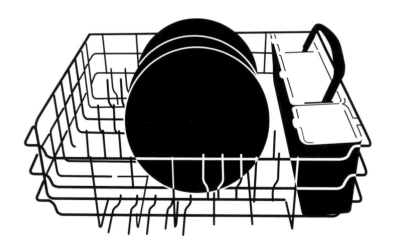

- To clean your **dishwasher**, place a cup of white vinegar into the bottom of the appliance and operate through an entire cycle. Do this once a month to reduce soap build up on the inner rollers, racks, gaskets, and sprayers.

- By wiping with a white vinegar dampened cloth, safely clean and shine **stainless steel** around your home and in your kitchen.

- Add a cup of white vinegar to a sink of warm water to clean your fine **china**, **crystal**, and **glassware**. Dip the item in the solution, rinse with warm water, and allow to air dry.

- To get stains and baked on "ick" out of **pots** and **pans**, fill the offending receptacle with three tablespoons of white vinegar and a pint of water. Allow the mixture to boil on your stovetop until the stain or "goo" loosens. Pour the mixture down the drain, then wash the rest away with soap and water.

- Boil a quarter-cup of white vinegar and one cup of water in a glass or plastic container in your **microwave** for two minutes. The condensation from the boiling mixture will loosen splattered-on food and those mysterious cheesy lumps, and will even deodorize the machine in the process. Wipe the inside clean with a damp cloth or sponge.

- Periodically, pour a cup of white vinegar into your **washing machine**. Allow it to operate through a regular cycle with no clothes added. This will dissolve soap residue from the drum of your machine and will keep it running smoothly for years.

- To prevent greasy **oven** buildup in the first place, dip a sponge in full-strength white vinegar and wipe down the entire **oven**, inside and out.

- Stop unpleasant **cooking odors** from permeating your house. Simply boil two cups of white vinegar in a pot on the stovetop. The vinegar will absorb the offending odors.

- Soak a towel in white vinegar. Wring it out and swing it around the room to remove the odor of **smoke** from the air. This works for smoke from tobacco as well as badly burned toast!

- To clean an automatic drip **coffeemaker**, run full-strength white vinegar through a normal brew cycle. Rinse by running plain water through the cycle twice. The pot will be remarkably clean and your coffee will taste better than ever. (Tip: Coffee sometimes tastes bitter because of soapy residue; therefore never wash your pot with soap.)

- Scour your **bathroom sink** and **tub** with full-strength white vinegar. Apply it with a sponge or a cloth and wipe it clean. It will remove that ugly **soap scum** ring.

- Clean your **ceramic tiles** with a solution of one-quarter cup white vinegar to one gallon warm water. Expect a miraculous shine.

- To remove **hard water spots** on your **tub**, **shower door**, and **shower stall**, apply full-strength white vinegar, wipe, let stand for five minutes, and then rinse with clean water. They will look as good as new.

- Clean up accidentally spilled white **glue** with white vinegar.

- **Deodorize your car** by soaking a piece of bread in white vinegar. Place it in a bowl or on a plate and leave it in the car overnight.

- Soak your rusty **tools** in white vinegar for a few hours or overnight. If needed, change the vinegar as it becomes cloudy.

- To remove **grass stains**, mix one-third cup white vinegar and two-thirds cup water. Apply the solution to the stain and blot with a clean cloth. Repeat the process, as needed, then wash as usual.

- Keep **lint** from clinging to your dark clothes by adding one-half cup white vinegar to the rinse cycle. (Check first for fiber content and if fabric is colorfast.)

- Use white vinegar to get rid of the **hard water deposits** around your sink. Soak a clean cloth with white vinegar and place it around the area that needs to be cleaned. Allow it to sit overnight. Rinse and wipe clean.

- Get your **grout** clean with full-strength white vinegar. Scrub with a toothbrush. (This sounds kind of obsessive but it works.)

• Two drops of white vinegar in your laundry will keep your **colors nice and bright**. (Relax, just two drops aren't gonna hurt anything.)

• Add a quarter-cup of white vinegar to rinse water to remove soapy or oily film from **laminate**, **Formica surfaces**, or **Corian**® **counters**. (Keep in mind that vinegar will create pits in "real" marble surfaces.)

- Rinse **jars** and **containers** with white vinegar to eliminate odors of previous contents.

- When rinsing **dishes** in a sink of hot water, add a capful of white vinegar to your rinse water to cut **grease** or **excess soap**. Your dishes will sparkle.

- Eliminate the smell of **cigarettes** or **paint** by placing a small bowl of white vinegar in a room. Leave it overnight and replace it the next day if needed.

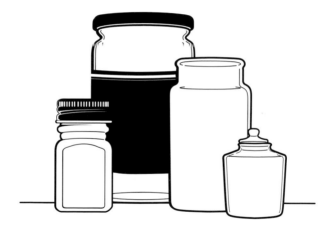

- Fill a spray bottle with white vinegar to chase away **ants**. They hate it.

- Remove **salt stains** from your shoes by wiping them with equal parts white vinegar and water.

- Get rid of **deodorant** and **antiperspirant residue** on washables by lightly rubbing the spots with white vinegar before washing. (Again, check labels for content and colorfastness.)

- Unclog any soap-scum formations from your **washing machine** by pouring a gallon of white vinegar in the washer tub and running it full cycle.

- After washing a **wool sweater** by hand, rinse in a quarter-cup of white vinegar and a sink of water to remove any additional odors. Rinse again with clean water.

- Pour white vinegar on any **unwanted grasses** (or **weeds**) for their swift elimination, especially in crevices and in between bricks.

- Clean **plastic** and **cloth shower curtains** in the washing machine. Add one cup of white vinegar to the rinse cycle to help deter mold and mildew.

Zen-Cleansing Recipes

Potions, inventions and concoctions . . . a pinch of this and a pinch of that. When mixing any of the fab-five Zen-Cleansing ingredients (baking soda, borax, lemon, salt, and vinegar), you create a recipe for a wholesome, healthy, and natural clean.

Shakespeare wrote of potions made and potions offered to miraculous and consequential effect. You, too, can expect a bit of magic—bubbles rising and cloudy swirling waters—while you clean. Channel the witches of Macbeth while you rinse a pot, wash the floor, or scrub your tub. Become a Mary Magdalene, a Mr. Belvedere, a Hazel, or a Mr. French by purifying your home with baptismal zeal. Pretend that you're Mr. Clean™ or a domestic goddess of the household arts. And always remember to take pride in your magical (and sometimes muscular) power to clean.

Allow the preparations that follow to become your personal springboard for thoughtful cleaning creativity. Since the fab-five ingredients are harmless*, use these proven recipes and potions to create your own Zen-Cleansing arsenal.

*But please, don't eat the borax! While the other four ingredients are actually used in cooking, borax should never be consumed.

Some Basic Zen-Cleansing Recipes

- Equal parts of borax, baking soda, and Ivory soap flakes makes amazing **laundry soap**. Store in a sealed glass jar. You'll never use anything else.

- To unclog a **drain**, pour a handful of baking soda down the drain and add one-half cup of white vinegar. Rinse with hot water.

- Replace your electric **dishwasher soap** with equal parts baking soda and borax. By adding a splash of white vinegar to the rinse cycle, stemware and glasses are sure to be extra shiny.

- Two parts olive oil mixed with one part lemon juice will make great **furniture polish**. Just a few drops on a soft cloth will get your wood furniture to shine. Store in a glass jar.

- Clean your oven without caustic or dangerous chemicals by sprinkling its cooled interior with baking soda and then applying lemon juice. Watch the **oven cleaner** bubble and let it sit for an hour. Clean with fresh water and a cloth.

- By cleaning with equal parts baking soda and white vinegar, your **toilet bowl** will be fresh and clean.

- To add to the longevity of fresh cut **flowers**, add two tablespoons white vinegar and one teaspoon sugar for each quart of water.

- Remove **fish**, **garlic**, or **onion odors** from your **hands** by rubbing them with a lemon wedge dipped in salt, and then rinsing with water.

117

- Remove **mineral deposits** and **debris** from a **glass flower vase** by mixing one-third cup salt and two tablespoons white vinegar to form a paste. Apply to inside of vase and let it stand 20 minutes, then scrub. Rinse vase and dry.

- Clear the air with a homemade **air freshener.** Just cut a lemon in half, remove pulp, and fill the peel with salt. It will provide a pleasant, aromatic lemony scent anywhere in your home.

- **Remove rust** from household tools and chrome by using salt and one tablespoon of lemon juice. Create a paste, apply to the rusted area with a dry cloth, and rub.

- Mix one-quarter cup borax and one-quarter cup baking soda to make the best **bathroom** and **kitchen cleanser** ever. Add some salt as an abrasive, if necessary.

- To remove stains on your **Formica counter** tops, squeeze fresh lemon juice on the spots and let it sit for 30 minutes. Sprinkle with baking soda, then scrub with a sponge. Rinse with clean water and wipe dry.

- Eliminate smelly odors from your **chopping block** by sprinkling baking soda on it, and then adding white vinegar. Let the two sizzle and bubble, then rinse clean. This is also a swell way to clean your sink and tub.

- Make a baking soda-water paste and rub it onto soiled or stained collars and armpits before washing, as a **laundering prewash**. Add a little white vinegar to stubborn stains (but first check the labels: do not use on cotton, linen, and garments that are not colorfast). Follow by washing as usual.

- For a fresh, **deodorized refrigerator**, leave an open box of baking soda or even a bowl of cut lemons on the shelf.

- Getting rid of odor from a **fire** is difficult. Wash walls and surfaces with a mixture of white vinegar and lemon diluted in water. Wash smoked-damaged clothing five times (yes, I said *five*) and add one-half cup each of white vinegar and baking soda to the rinse cycle every time.

- Sprinkle baking soda on whatever **surface** you want to clean. Next, add white vinegar to the baking soda. If you need to make it more powerful, just add a little borax.

- To remove **mildew** from just about anything, use equal parts of white vinegar and borax.

- For an **all-purpose liquid cleaner**, combine equal amounts of white vinegar and borax.

- For stubborn **bath stains** or **kitchen stains**, clean surfaces by using a mixture of lemon juice and borax. Scrub with an abrasive pad. Rinse with clean water.

- Lemon juice or salt makes a good all-purpose **spot remover**.

122

- For stains on either **porcelain** dishes or **bath** and **kitchen fixtures**, rub with a sliced lemon dipped into salt to remove the stains.

- To whiten **yellowed cotton** and **linen fabrics**, add one-quarter cup each of baking soda and salt to your largest enamel pot and fill with water. Boil fabrics under a watchful eye for about an hour.

- Dip half a lemon into borax to create a **basin**, **tub**, and **tile cleaner**. Scrub using the halved lemon, juicy side down. Rinse with clean water.

- To clean a **noncoated pan** with a burnt-on mess, boil a mixture of equal parts white vinegar and baking soda right in the pan.

- Polish **copper pans** with a half a lemon dipped into salt. Rub in a circular motion and then rinse in clear water. Repeat until the copper shines. (A mix of vinegar and salt also works well.)

- To clean your **brass**, make a paste with equal parts white vinegar, flour, and salt. Leave on for an hour, and then buff with soft cloth.

- To get pesky, persistent **tomato stains** (or stains from spices, herbs, etc.) out of your **plastic storage containers**, scrub them using combinations of lemon juice, baking soda, and white vinegar. (Note: Elbow grease required, and this one ain't guaranteed! Remember—it isn't your family heirloom china.)

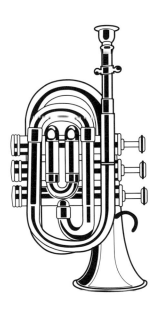

. . . .

Live life to the fullest. Respect the physical . . . be in the moment.

1. Clean a little every day . . . the best way to devour an elephant is by eating it one slow bite at a time.

2. There's no reason to clean alone. Drag a lover, neighbor, spouse, child, parent, or pet into the act. It's always better with two.

3. Anybody can clean. (No excuses.)

4. Clean with thoughtful consideration and significance. Lose yourself in the ordinary, and by doing so, infuse it with meaning.

5. Not everything needs cleaning. A little (very little) grime can sometimes be swell.

6. Prioritize. If a must-see movie, short-lived play, or an exhibition or concert recital stands between you and clean living, opt for culture.

7. At a certain point, any space can only get so dirty—don't obsess. If your schedule doesn't allow you to clean weekly, then do it bimonthly. In the scheme of things, nobody will really notice the difference.

8. Your home is a reflection of who you are. It's a gift to those around you each time you care to plan, organize, entertain, cook, and clean.

9. For every action there's a reaction. When you clean, expect something marvelous in return.

10. Fix it, change it, clean it, make it better, or get rid of it.

11. Why clean? Why ask?

Acknowledgments

CLEAN would not have been possible were it not for the suggestions, support, encouragement, and talents of the following people, whom I want to thank from the bottom of my heart:

My mom, Ruth De Jong

My brother, John, and twin sister, Mags

My partner for life, Richard Haymes

Matthew Waldman and his talented design team at Berrymatch

The incomparable Joost Elffers, my publisher and friend, and the anonymous cab driver who brought us together

Michael De Jong is an artist who spends
most of his time in and around New York City.

The CLEAN® logo

© Michael De Jong and Joost Elffers Books